Simon the Shepherd Boy of Bethlehem

Copyright © 2018 by Jim Metcalf
All world rights reserved.

Illustrations by Shannon Maisel.

No part of this book may be reproduced, stored in a retrieval system, or transmitted in any form or by any means electronic, mechanical, photocopying, recording or otherwise, without the prior consent of the publisher.

Readers are encouraged to go to www.MissionPointPress.com to contact the author or to find information on how to buy this book in bulk at a discounted rate.

Published by Mission Point Press
2554 Chandler Rd.
Traverse City, MI 49686
(231) 421-9513
www.MissionPointPress.com

ISBN: 978-1943995745

Printed in the United States of America.

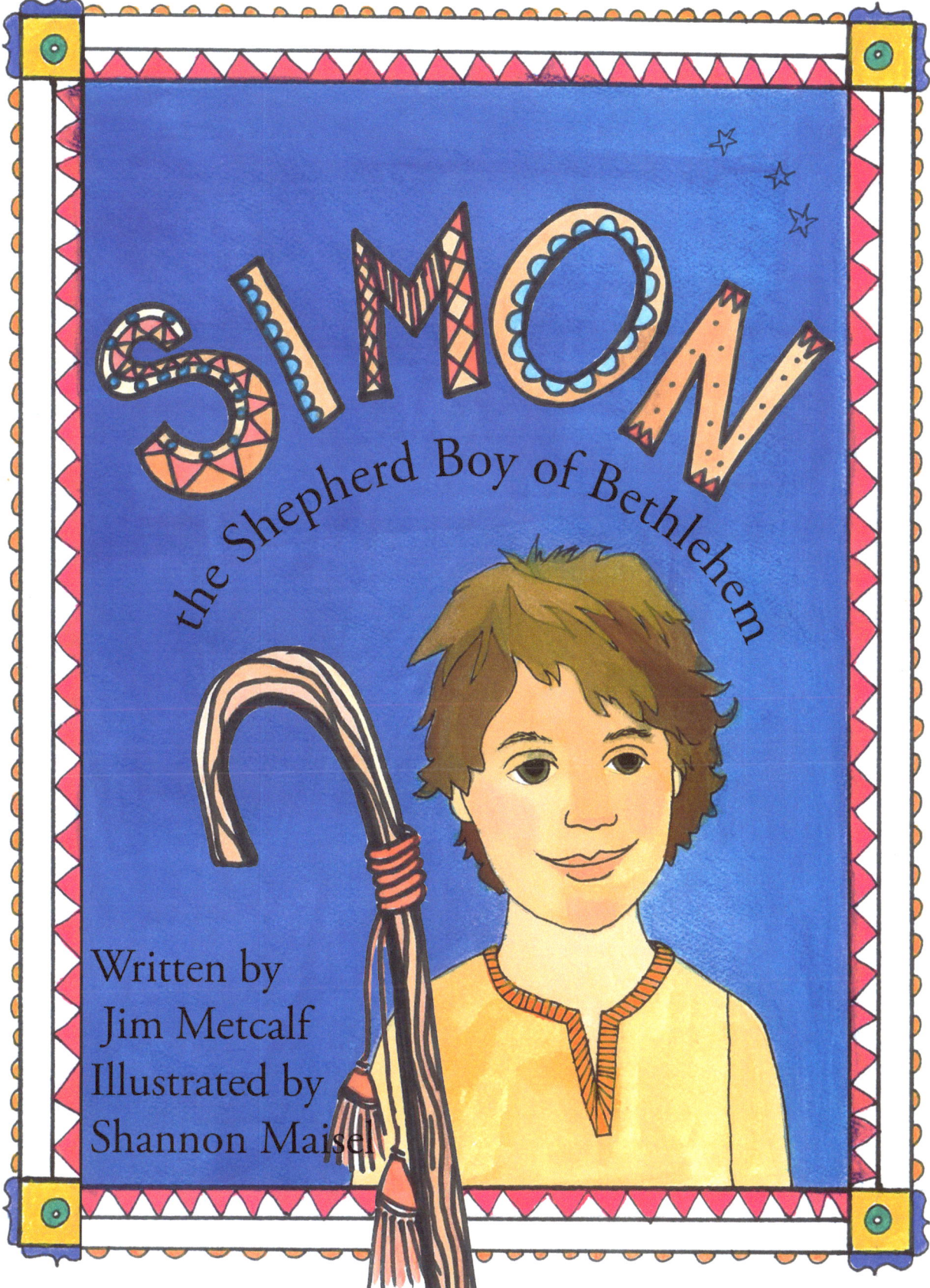

Author's Note

The classic Christmas story in the Gospel according to St. Luke tells us that Joseph and Mary "found no room in the inn." The word translated as "inn" in the King James Version ("kataluma" in Greek) is later translated as "guest chamber" in Luke's story of the Last Supper, and this is a much better translation. There were no inns in Bethlehem. It was too small and too far from Roman roads. Besides, inns were too disreputable for a good Jewish village like Bethlehem, and certainly for a nice couple like Joseph and Mary. Significantly, the 2010 version of the NIV also translates "kataluma" as "guest room" in the Christmas story.

Families in Palestinian villages such as Bethlehem lived in very small homes, often only a single room. The animals were stabled on the ground floor and the people lived on an elevated platform that had mangers for the animals carved into the edge. The total size might be at most a couple of hundred square feet. When a family grew older, larger or richer, a second room was added. Sometimes the room was on the roof of the house and sometimes it was to the side. This was the guest room, or "kataluma".

When Joseph and Mary arrived in Bethlehem, they were not the first guests to come back home. Every guest room in Bethlehem was already occupied. No problem! Hospitality was a great virtue in these villages. Honor was at stake. So, the young couple was invited to move in with a family in the main room. They did.

As I imagine the story, the family in the guest room of the house where Joseph and Mary were living is the family of a man named Zebedee, a brother of the house's owner. He had gone north to Galilee, settled in Capernaum, become a fisherman, and started a family. Now, like so many others who had gone to Galilee, he was back in Bethlehem to pay the tax and be counted in the census. His young sons were with him. Their names are James and John. His brother's sons are Simon and Andrew.

"Simon, get going!"

"I don't want to go, Dad, sheep are boring!"

"Sheep are boring, huh? So, you want to go fishing instead?"

"Can I? Can I? Fishing's fun. Sheep are boring."

"Keep it up, Simon, and you'll go fishing alright. I'll send you home with your Uncle Zebedee. You can fish for him all night, every night on the Sea of Galilee. Now, get going. It's your turn to help watch the sheep."

"But Dad, there's nothing to do, nothing to see out there."

"You can watch the stars while you tend the sheep. You can't stay here tonight. Mary's having her baby. It's time to go. Andrew and your cousins are waiting."

"Mary's having her baby? I've never seen a baby born before."

"Sorry, Simon," said Mary. "Having babies is women's work. Watching sheep is man's work, most of the time anyhow. You can see my baby in the morning. He will either be in my arms or lying here in the manger."

So, Simon left his cozy house in Bethlehem to catch up with his brother and cousins.

"C'mon, Simon! Hurry up. The others are waiting for us."

That was Andrew. He was always looking out for him. Simon liked Andrew. He was like their father, quiet and kind.

So, Simon ran a bit and then the two brothers jogged together to catch up to James and John at the edge of Bethlehem. The sheepfold wasn't far from the village this early in the season. Soon they were all there. The young boys chatted a bit with their older friends, who would be returning to the village after a long day.

"We haven't seen any wolves or bears, but stay awake anyhow. The sheep are restless tonight. Don't know why. Maybe there's something going on we can't figure out. Keep your eyes open. You never know what you might see. We'll be back early in the morning so you can get some sleep."

Then the older boys headed for home, leaving their sheep with the younger boys, bedded down in the fold outside of town that they used in the warmer days of the rainy season.

The four young boys walked around the perimeter of the sheepfold, checking the sheep. They said nothing. Sleeping sheep were easier to care for than restless ones. No sense disturbing them.

 But at last Andrew spoke quietly. He was the oldest. "We have four watches — each of us takes one. Off watch, we'll spread out. You sleep there, James. John, over there. I'll take the far side, farthest from the village. Simon, you stay awake and walk the edge of the sheepfold until that star is over your head. Then wake me up and it's my turn."

"There'll be nothing to see, Andrew. There's nothing to see out here but wool on the grass."

"You never know," said Andrew.

Simon began to walk. At first, he imagined he was circling Jericho, waiting for the walls to fall down. Then he thought he was David, circling Goliath.

He reached for his sling. It was there, hanging from his belt. Then he looked for lions in the dark. No lions. He breathed a sigh of relief. He felt for his sling again. "I can take anyone with this sling," he thought.

"Anything! Just like David!" he thought. "I'm so powerful with this old sling. I could whip a wolf. Heck, I could bruise a bear, even lick a lion. With this sling I could. I can beat anything! Anyone!" At last he looked for the stars. Was his star overhead yet?

Now Simon was sleepy. The star seemed to be moving just a little.

"It's just a star," he thought. "There's never anything to see out here."

And then, just then, when it was nearly midnight ... an angel appeared! Now, Simon didn't know it was an angel. He had never, ever seen an angel before. He did know that his sling wasn't going to help him this time. Suddenly, he did not feel so powerful. Lions, bears and wolves were one thing. This was something entirely else.

His knees shook. His hands trembled. His voice stuck in his throat. He couldn't call Andrew. He couldn't call his cousins. Nothing would come out of his mouth, but it didn't matter. The others were awake — the angel made a tremendously bright light all around them. And the angel spoke. It was the most beautiful, most musical voice Simon had ever heard.

"Don't be afraid," the angel said. "I have only good news for you, great and joyful news. News for everyone! Your Savior has just been born in Bethlehem. He is Christ the Lord. You'll know him this way: He is an infant, wrapped in cloth and lying in a manger."

"Lying in a manger?" thought Simon. "That's just what Mary said."

Suddenly the sky was filled with angels. The bright light grew brighter still. The voice grew louder and more musical yet. "Glory in the highest heavens to God, and on earth, peace among good hearted people." That's what they sang, and then they were gone.

"Did you see that, Andrew? Did you see that? I kept my eyes open just like you said. Boy, I saw it! Did you see it? Did you hear them?"

"I saw it! Sure, I saw it! Did you see it, boys? They'll never believe this back in Bethlehem."

"Bethlehem!" shouted Simon. "Mary's had her baby! We have to go see it! We have to!"

"What about the sheep?"

"Leave 'em or bring 'em. Nothing, no one's going to bother them tonight. There's big stuff going on," said Andrew. "I don't know what it is, but I saw it. I've never seen anything like it!" He paused. "The sheep will be alright tonight. Our God's got us all covered."

Simon, Andrew, the others, they all ran to Bethlehem, right to the home of Simon and Andrew.

Simon's dad met them at the door. "Hey," he said. "What …?"

"We saw angels, Dad. Didn't you hear them? They were singing. They said a baby was born. They said …"

"It's all right. Let the boys in. The sheep will be fine." It was Mary speaking. And in fact, the sheep had followed their shepherds back into the village. The boys crowded into the home. The sheep tried crowding in, too.

There was a baby lying in the sheep's manger. He was wrapped in cloths. Mary looked both tired and happy.

Joseph was lost in thought. "Angels," he murmured. "Angels," he said again, more loudly. "You saw angels? What did they say? What did they look like?"

Simon told him everything. He told him about being bored and about his dreams of killing powerful lions or bears or wolves with his sling, just like David did before he was king.

He told him about being afraid when he saw the angel, and about his fear leaving just as quickly when the angel told him this baby was Christ the Lord.

Joseph just nodded.

"Well, say something, Joseph! It's your baby!"

"No. He's not my baby," said Joseph. "He's ours because He's God's. I can't understand it myself, so you'll just have to believe me when I tell you this. The things we don't see, or seldom see, like angels, are more powerful than the things we can see, like lions and bears and wolves.

"Think of your father loving you, for example, or your brother being kind to you. And then, once in a great while, the things we see are not all that they seem to be. What looks powerful is really weak. What looks tiny, small, just like a baby, is Lord of all. This baby is Lord of all. The angel told me so. We'll just have to believe it. We only have the Word we've heard."

Mary was listening to her husband. And she treasured all these things in her heart.

www.ingramcontent.com/pod-product-compliance
Lightning Source LLC
Chambersburg PA
CBHW041722040426
42451CB00003B/24